once upon a twin

once upon a twin

raymond luczak

Gallaudet University Press
Washington, DC

Gallaudet University Press
Washington, DC 20002
gupress.gallaudet.edu

ISBN 978-1-944838-76-8 (paperback)
ISBN 978-1-944838-77-5 (ebook)

Library of Congress Cataloging-in-Publication Data

Names: Luczak, Raymond, 1965– author.
Title: Once upon a twin : poems / Raymond Luczak.
Description: Washington, DC: Gallaudet University Press, [2021] | Summary:
    "When Raymond Luczak was growing up deaf in a hearing family of nine
    children, his mother shared conflicting stories about having had a
    miscarriage after-or possibly around-the time he was conceived. As an
    elegy to his lost twin, this book asks: if he had a twin, just how
    different would his life have been?"— Provided by publisher.
Identifiers: LCCN 2020033501 (print) | LCCN 2020033502 (ebook) | ISBN
    9781944838768 (paperback) | ISBN 9781944838775 (ebook)
Subjects: LCGFT: Poetry.
Classification: LCC PS3562.U2554 O53 2021  (print) | LCC PS3562.U2554
    (ebook) | DDC 811/.54—dc23
LC record available at https://lccn.loc.gov/2020033501
LC ebook record available at https://lccn.loc.gov/2020033502

Cover: Front and back cover image by William Blake (1757–1827). *Angel of the Revelation*, ca.
1803–5. Watercolor, pen, and black ink, over traces of graphite, 15 7/16 x 10 1/4 in. (39.2 x 26
cm.). The Rogers Fund, 1914 (14.81.4). The Metropolitan Museum of Art, New York, NY, USA.
Work is licensed under CC0 1.0. metmuseum.org/art/collection/search/340852

Cover design: Mona Z. Kraculdy.

Author photograph by Raymond Luczak
© 2020 by Raymond Luczak

∞ This paper meets the requirements of ANSI/NISO Z39.48-1992 (Permanence of Paper).

*in memoriam*

TODD WILLIAM CARLBORN
1964–2008

# contents

## ironwood (1976–1981)

## twinhood

## houghton (1974–1976)

## kyrie

\*

\*

"Despair is a very difficult thing. I think I have to be reborn."
—Antoine de Saint-Exupery (1900–1944)

# 9 months

mom still wonders how i lost my hearing
she mentions having a miscarriage in april 65
& being surprised to find herself pregnant again
in june 65 dr santini said id be born in january 66
instead i arrived in november 65 fully formed
not a preemie i go home two days later

\*

not long after my sister carole takes
to reading out loud from a book
she is learning how to read to me
as i am trapped in my crib
i have apparently cocked my ears
to her voice laboriously decoding words

\*

then mom changes her story
she remembers having a miscarriage in march 65
it fell out of her while she sat on the toilet
at 16 i constantly wondered
if that was indeed possible
a body expelling her own fetus like that

\*

a heatwave in july 66
i turn pink & hot but everybody is hot anyway
mom wonders maybe somethings seriously wrong
at the hospital i am found to have double pneumonia
& a high fever i look close to dying so a priest is called in
i survive my last rites of death but my hearing doesnt

*

then mom changes details again
she says she had a d&c done in february 65
when she felt her fetus wasnt growing
it wasnt even 2 centimeters long
no idea whether it was a boy or girl
i am no longer sure what to believe

*

after i come back home from the hospital
carole reads to me again
this time i bob my head around
she doesnt realize ive lost most of my hearing
no one has either
she gets frustrated with me & gives up

*

by the time i turn 2 & a half
mom asks her doctor why i havent begun talking
he says well maybe hes deaf she comes home
& tells dad whos been washing me he stands me up
& turns me around so i can face the wall above the tub
i dont respond to my name

&ast;

research indicates a twin in the womb could miscarry
leaving behind its other half overlooked
in the 60s technology hadnt existed to detect
such a tiny baby
thats why moms pregnancy test results in june 65
had so surprised everyone

&ast;

up & down oak street where i once roamed
the trees are mostly gone
but the shadow of my other half
still runs a mean yellow stripe
right through the road of my life
the mystery of never knowing him

ironwood
(1976–1981)

# my corpse self

alone in these woods
across the street from moms house
trails worn down became boundaries
of a country with no name
it would take me many years to walk
this meandering path across
peat concrete grill escalator airplane elevator aisle
in between waited for clarifications
the only thing found in morass of trees & grasses
was my shadow barely alive
panting for my kiss
sleeping forlorn prince
he looked familiar but nothing like a reflection
my watery self not even close
tall & lanky with a mask made with wood
stained & polished with veneer
perfected from years pretending to be happy
while people took him down behind his back
threw tiny paper balls at him
always feigning innocence who me
surely you jest their faces all said
i looked down at
his lax skeleton in a faux shroud of turin
his body spotted with grays like leopard gone starved
i didnt want to hold him
i didnt want weight of his troubles
when in my shoes a sea
pebbles a relentless reminder
puncturing each step walked for miles
couldnt a shadow be light easily blown away
like how people dismissed me with a glance
just like my hearing family & classmates
constantly cleaved
mortar slabbed onto bricks
until my face turned unreadable
now his
there in my arms

the darkness of him
transparent
bright shining eyes
begging me to save him
alone in these woods

## first prayer

woods across    street    no markers

for    dead    trapped in    dank tunnels

collapsed    water surging    chunks    iron ore

my tenners could never shake free    powder rust-soil

past lives murmuring among    grasses just beyond

cave-ins    half-buried graves    mineshafts

shadows outlined    cartographers dreaming together

measuring    walking back    starting again

rust-colored coins    prosperity    now stones

winds teasing me ghosts    no name

stalking me    trying    whisper stories

tall figures flickering among    birches

leaves    tiny blades flip-turning

breeze kept shouting my name

kept turning    hoping    find someone there

hands clasped in prayer    would open    release

crows    fluttering    black answers

inking    november skies

## battle preparations

mercury dropping
our thermometer
outside porch window
framing st michaels
rising above birches
those mornings
my universe was
a stretched atlas
of silver & white
patches worn thin
over edge of ironing board
there my shirt lay
mangled corpse
stripes & angles
misted with elixir water
hot button steam
warm as bloodstains
straightening collar
like a priest ready
to officiate
death rites
before burial
iron pressing a prayer
flattening chest pockets
weaving around buttons
medaled down the front
shirttails now wings
tucked inside my pants
hiding my body hearing aids
still a perfect soldier
no wrinkles or lintballs
still at boot camp
with those odd things in my ears
after so many sessions
speech therapy
three times a week
a weird flat accent that never

pinpointed the country
of my nasalities
taught me pay close attention
supposed to lipread better
but kept decoding body language
seemingly encrypted in cipher
easy code to break
my superiors whispering
among themselves
as they tossed footballs
to each other
glancing my way
just me in shirt & pants
standing guard
by brick wall
uniformed or not
unarmed with only
imperfect consonants
no rifle in hand
still dangerous

## the easiest words to lipread in a schoolyard
## (even if you're not deaf)

asshole
battybat
big baby
blundering boob
boobs
bj
crazy
crybaby
cuckoo
damn
deaf & dumb
dick
dumbdumb
fag
foureyes
funny
hey you
mental up here
pussy
queer
retard
sicko
showoff
stupid
you girlie

## gods copper

every sunday at st michaels    all of us nine kids sat in the fourth pew    so
i could lipread father frank better    yet his voice was so whispery    with
no facial expression    after mass he always glanced down at me    &
ignored me as he carried on with mom & dad    hed married them back
in 57    i fidgeted with my siblings    waiting to pile into dads station
wagon & go over    to grandmas house on greenbush street    wed run
pellmell    screaming & laughing through her house    maybe id bang on
the upright piano    but always grandma stood as if an angel fronted with
an apron    with the aura of sun through the pantry window    she picked
out a shiny penny & pressed it onto my palm    as she looked deep into my
eyes    she somehow understood i didnt need words    just some unfiltered
communication    her blue eyes looking into mine    with her liverspotted
hand on mine    i lived for every sunday morning knowing    i did truly
matter not just another mouth to feed    not just a quiet boy waiting to say
something    then she fell because of a stroke    in that limbo atmosphere
of silence & death    i prayed to god begging to bring her back    wasnt
god supposed to love me too    instead i burned with copper in my veins

# deaf rich boy 79

i would one day be the son of that rich man
with a monocle found in the game of monopoly
id own the entire town beyond pamida
i wouldnt think twice about buying
a pair of expensive designer jeans at the down under shop
at stern & field on aurora & suffolk
all the kids in my class would ask meekly to see
my latest handheld electronic game
the kind that you couldnt find anywhere
the kind that kids would know everything about
the kind that theyd grow antennae just to ferret them out
theyd turn into insects with shiny shellbacks
gleaming with bands of gold strapped across
as they murmured & compared between themselves
their dull scores blinking tiny sticks of red light
theyd huddle together & forget about everything
id wear the latest nike sneakers from jcpenneys
the kind none of the kids could afford
theyd stare & gawk at me of all people
when theyd thought me poor
what with eight siblings & a dog packed
into a house of only four bedrooms
my family werent rich
everybody knew that
but on that first day of school id say nothing
as i hung my denim trucker jacket on my hook
in the hallway theyd see the name furstenberg
stitched on the back pocket of my new jeans
id be wearing a blondie tshirt to show off the fact
that i went to minneapolis to see
the sultry debbie harry sing heart of glass
for once the hearing aid cords winding up to my ears
would look cool as if i were always listening
to something cool that theyd never hear
always straining to hear the next hot band
id hear them way before they appeared
on american bandstand some saturday afternoon

theyd wish to be deaf like me
always listening to the future
these kids in class would whisper about me
never mocking me but always with awe

## the tiniest snakes

cackling
                                                    &
                                                                     hissing
away
braided
                      in
                                               beige
scales
weaving
                      up
                                           from
                      my
electric
                      boobies
                                      boxed
                      inside
white
                      against
                                      white
                   undershirt
hooked
                      onto
                                      the
                      cusps
of
                      my
                                      ears
ready
                      to
                                    devour
                      more
than
                      earwax
                                      deep
                      in

my
            canals
                        would
            surely
sneak
            into
                        the
            apple
halves
            of
                        my
            brain
&
            unleash
                        that
            horrible
bang
            louder
                        than
            a
cannonball
            scorching
                        off
            therefore
knowledge
            of
                        how
            to
lie
            cheat
                        bully
            like
every
            hearing
                        boy
            i
knew
            thus
                        ruptured

                    i
would
            turn
                        into
            a
tree
            its
                    roots
        clawing
at
            the
                    earth
        trying
forever
            more
                        to
            kill
those
            slimy
                    beasts
            who
broke
            into
                        the
            shiny
stainless
            steel
                    boxes
        thought
safe
            in
                    my
        bosom

ONCE UPON A TWIN

## the mighty thurible

i was too secretly pissed off to be like jesus   no one told me the mathematical formula for converting hatred into love the kind of love that jesus would give in spite of being punched on the jaw & kicked about on the ground i didnt want anyone to see the bones trying to cage in my vile black heart throbbing   being subservient didnt help defend me against them boys   i wanted to hide my growing spite with my black cassock & white surplice with badlyfitting shoes   when we served as altar boys at st michaels there were 10 pairs of black shoes to choose from so some of us had to show up quite early   no sneakers were allowed up there so if a pair of black shoes didnt quite fit our feet we had to make do by walking very slowly sometimes i slid my feet across the crimson carpet for fear of hearing that clucking sound when the bottom of my shoes slapped my feet as i carried a brass thurible swaying incense down the aisle & around the pews & back to the altar   i tried to suppress my own coughs as tiny fish hooks of smoke dug into my mouth demanding that i open my mouth to swallow it all

\*

i kept wondering why i had to give father h a dime out of my own 50 cent weekly allowance when he owned a black cadillac parked next to the rectory   my dad needed a better station wagon   it never occurred to me back then if father h was indeed a true christian hed have insisted that dad take his cadillac to sell & use the money to buy a better car for transporting us 9 kids   father h stood pontificating away secure in knowing that no one would learn then what the la times newspaper would finally reveal 8 years after hed died in 2005   the la diocese was forced to release his name among the 24 more priests who were credibly accused of sexual abuse  if he were alive today hed have been hunted down like a nazi criminal lingering somewhere in brazil   instead father h got to retire far away to the mesas of arizona   he got away with the sins of entitlement

*

just like joanna cameron uttering o mighty isis when in need of her goddess powers every saturday morning on tv id spin the incensechoked thurible above my head its atomic clouds spewing & swirling tightly before spiraling outward until the skies above us were candystriped in gray    thunder & lightning would come shatter the immaculate bowl of sky raining down thick droplets of ash turning into snowflakes   the land everywhere would turn not white but the same gray   buildings & cars & people would be in the same monochromatic gray too   each movement would outline them even the headlights would be the same color   no one could see a foot ahead of themselves   itd be worse than the infamous london fog of yore   the grayness would fill the air with incense constantly burning never going out & driving everyone mad with the desire to put it out but no one could ever pinpoint where to squelch that back of the throat itch   id fill the thurible with the most fragrant rose petals & spin it above my head spuming forth that scent & clearing the infinite window of air like a rag infused with windex   everyone on the street would stop & stare at the color of my cassock no longer a matte black but a shimmering gold just like king tuts death mask   theyd fall to their knees   one day i would be made king with my shoes fitting perfectly

## atonement

hoping that like in the gaudilyframed print
of jesus holding out his stigmata palms
amidst clouds swirling around him
high on the wall opposite me
in the bedroom off the kitchen
a warm beam of light would break
showing the garage outside
a flashlight shining down on me
clouds whooshing in
through that crack of wall
elevating me
my clothes suddenly a tangle of folds
arms holding up like branches
looking down on faces
the ones whod made me weep
turning my heart into pewter
smiling forth in my beatification
theyd never know how much id longed
see them suffer make them kneel
before me a boy gifted with hearing aids
beg for mercy from god who never listened
just like how hed never listened
angels would descend with their hands
stealing away everyones voices
flinging them far away
beyond the sun
streaks of light dissipating
as my hands would whisper
this is how you must speak now

# heretics

sign language was a sin
for us deaf people
learning to speak
how silly was that
anything forbidden
becomes even more desired
like nothing else
so when gramps morrison sat
in front of the iron inn tavern
on aurora street he fingerspelled
to anyone who wanted to learn
mom forced me not to look
whenever we passed
but oh such sweet stolen glances
his movements were mysterious
as those dreams that bobbed
like apples on the water
impossible to catch with our teeth
always taunting me
but no matter
there he was
a torch in the tunnel
more powerful than any
biblical proclamation
amplified on any microphone
or on any tv screen
sitting there
not acting anything special
yet
he was both moses & jesus
the sky above st michaels
began showing fractures
traces of lightning
double exposed
my first time realizing
how i could worship
a language wholly ours

# the new baltimore catechism for the deaf

lines in my hands
clear as life itself
pure language
born inside us
gossamer threads
thinner than veins
spewing out of us
like staticky hair
electricity searing
whenever we open
our mouths
to preach
so many souls
yet to save
how it rains
softly warmly
when we turn off
the gurgly faucets
of our throats
our hands
would glow
like christmas lights
blinking
slowly as sigh
clarity would be
our new mass

# the other night when i died

woke up thinking    after having read up    what it was like to die    &
come back    see a warm tunnel    filled with people    used to know    before
they died    theyd tell me to go back    wake up    feeling saved    cleareyed
about my purpose    in life    better than any    religious nirvana    but
none of that    happened one winter night    tried to overdose    on 30 st
josephs    orangeflavored    childrens aspirins    watched myself    in the
big bathroom mirror    starting to feel cold    thought then    am gonna
die    this is it for sure    but no    just got cold & colder    gave up on
waiting    my family were in the living room    watching tv & laughing
went up the stairs    into the dark    my left hand    gripped the wood ball
crowning the rail at the top    lay there    under heavy blankets    waited
& waited    for death to come    take me away    far far far away    further
than anywhere    ever gone    further than marquette    that life thread of
mine    between body & soul    severed    floating like an aura    rushing
toward the sky    & never looking back    at the dull lights lining    my
street    the whole world    under my feet    would be spinning    like a
marble    just flicked off    with my thumb    toward a hole    carved out
of the hard soil    with our feet    the marbles colors    spinning in a blur
except that    my aura was the blur    searing underneath    the stars    a
wonder to behold    people on the ground    would exclaim    thats a
comet    never seen it coming    how come nobody warned me    well look
at that    but none of that happened    somehow fell asleep    dragging
my feet    in that cold land    of dreams frozen    forever trapped    inside

statues made of ice    not the kinda place    where summer would    drop

by & melt    the coldest of hearts    none of the statues    whispered

back    my dreams woke up at dawn    still cold    but the sun was

shining    had a new secret    in my bones    that kept me warm & powerful

# twinhood

# if you were my twin

would you stand up to them boys mocking me
& raise your fists
would you sit there in our principals office
our faces in double exposure
glumly staring back
at sister mary fidelias stern face framed by cateyes
she wouldnt want to hear how it all started
what mattered was that one of us used our hands
to inflict bodily damage against verbal damage
inflicted on me a deaf boy
of course she wouldnt punish them boys as badly
mom & dad would bow their heads in shame
cause wed failed them once again

mom would try over & over again to separate us
by seating us far apart from each other at the dinner table
you would listen for me what everyone was saying
youd fingerspell who was saying what was so funny
id finally laugh just like everyone else
you would smile knowing what would make me laugh
i would also look for things that make you laugh
nothing like seeing my best friend laughing so hard
rolling over on the living room carpet because
i was funny hysterically better than anyone in our family
nobody in my family would agree on that
you didnt care because i still made you chortle

would you have gone out there on the parking lot
shaming them boys into letting me join them
you & i wouldve created a language all our own
i could read any facial expression of yours
& know what i had to do to win the nerfball for our team
them boys would finally leave me alone
because messing around with me meant
messing around with you
youd stand proudly next to me by the brick wall

sometimes wed make plans for another biking trip
maybe wed set up a tent fashioned out of blankets
in the woods south of norrie park & watch
dragonflies & mosquitoes dance off the montreal river
curling around us toward north
toward lake superior
miles & miles ahead of our dreams
wed drink water from our plastic koolaid kanteen
wed eat moms molasses cookies
already hard to crack like thick glass
wed play old maid gin rummy go fish
while the sun dappled shadows & light
through the mottle of pine trees above us
wed never talk about them boys
being alone with you would be
a cake slice from heaven

# braided veins

as we grow up youd speculate this or that bully would probably grow to be bald & fat     id laugh at the notion saying it was not possible     after all them boys were so muscular     but you would be so wise beyond years youd tell me that im gay before i knew     you would say not to worry about what others think when it comes to the man i end up loving     they arent sleeping with him     you are so whys it a problem     you would tell me later that youre gay too     we would find it odd how similar our tastes in men are     our husbands would feel lonely & commiserate together now & then when they watch us jabber away in our alone time     we would constantly reassure them that we still loved them very much     but we are twins & twins have their own thing deeper than blood deeper than family deeper than love     we would always be thinking of each other no matter how far apart we are     we wouldnt think of each other by name just a presence lingering in our braided veins     we would know just when to text each other & when not to     we would know how to reassure our husbands when they are just like everyone else envious of our bond     we wouldnt dress the same     thats so childish     we would have our own individual lives     we would tire of strangers quizzing if it was true that we could read each others minds     we would trade glances & laugh yeah right but secretly there have been times we felt we could wed never tell anyone about those times     not even our own husbands     we would show up at our family reunions our siblings now fat & old would talk to you more than to me     hed remind them hey talk to him     hes my twin you know     my eyes would shoot daggers at their faces    didnt they get that fucking memo how family was supposed to love each other unconditionally no matter what just like how you & i love each other like brothers like best friends better than soulmates youd roll your eyes each time they tried to make a joke    by then youd have learned some asl    you wouldnt be that great with your signing but i would feel guilty in asking you to interpret for me what they were all saying not being fluent enough youd simply summarize    no more ill tell you laters & forgetting    after too many reunions where i was ignored youd tell everyone that you & i werent coming back ever because i didnt deserve being ignored    hes deaf so you guys fucking deal with it    you would storm out & id join you in your car while our husbands sat in the backseat id watch you drive with rage whitening your knuckles    id tell you that you didnt have to say that    youd say i dont care    the way they treat you like that still    our own family    fuck    later id join my husband in the backseat his hand would find mine    id feel like a found family all over again    your husband is always careful to slow down for me    he wouldnt be easy to lipread but i can tell hes so good for you    its so easy to forgive him as long as he tries to make himself clear    my dear husband would be deaf    youd always make a point of making him laugh with your silly facial expressions he too wouldve grown up in a hearing family like i have    he doesnt like them    he hadnt understood growing up how hearing families can be toxic sometimes you have to quit them cold turkey or do suicide    he doesnt like my family either    a true family is a group of people who totally get you    they dont look down on you or ignore you    they dont give you fake smiles when they see you    they dont ask you how are you doing & ignore you the rest of the evening   hey if you werent happy i wouldn't be happy

either   we look at each other our blood pulsing in the air between us

# fraternal identical

if i chanced upon you
in a dressing room mirror
at the back of s&l
trying on a sweater
id recoil from seeing
the nakedness of your chest
the weird hairs sprouting
between your nipples
its skin stretched taut
against bony ridges
id say youre not even a man
even though youre 16
like me
id run away from you

but if id grown up
with you as my twin
id have seen your body
many times
maybe wed have compared
ourselves
standing together
in the mirror
& noting the tiny variances
between our identical bodies
id never think
my body was ugly
at all
id feel fine just like you

# if my twin were a she

i wouldnt think of her as a she
either because seeing each other
    every day for so many hours
    wed stop seeing each other
as male & female
just each others half thats all
    no name really
    just a happy shadow
always nearby with a look
sometimes a question
    standing in the bathtub
    wed look at each others body
& go oh thats all so thats why i wouldnt
think of her as a her but the pronoun
    attached to her name
    but not her body itself
our parents would go hey
dont play barbie dolls with her
    thats not right for boys
    or they would go hey
dont plays tonka trucks with him
girls dont do that kind of stuff
    wed still talk & stuff
    but wed feel their gaze
as if wed do something abnormal
shed know that i was different
    just unable to put it into words
    i might say something about that boy
so nice & sweet but not yet knowing
that i could use words like cute
    shed go oh like it wasnt a big deal
    a few years later when puberty hits
id see her breasts develop
& her hips widen
    shed spend more time
    alone in the big bathroom

learning how to apply makeup
id go hey thats not you
    why do you have to put on that stuff
    youre fine as you are
id never tell her how id squirreled
away to examine my gawky body
    its tentative hairs slowly creeping
    lichen on the tree trunk of my body
down there too & why am i getting
hard when i see a nice man smile back
    so many silences would pass
    between us for years
we wouldnt know how to talk
about these things deep inside
    id feel sad when shed leave me behind
    to talk with our older sisters
about boys & dating & stuff
id hear them giggle among themselves
    while i wondered if it was possible
    for two guys to meet for like a date you know
id worry every time if she could smell
the scent of another guy mingling with my sweat
    in those days i sought sex in public restrooms
    their glances were full of loneliness too
we would be the closest of friends
for a few minutes before leaving the stall
    shed go off to a hearing college
    id go off to a deaf college & come out
our first christmas break id tell her
shed go oh yeah i always knew
    shed tell me about the guys she met
    wed compare notes about guys we dated
there will be moments when i forget
im not supposed to talk about these things
    with a straight woman but as a twin
    shed end up knowing everything anyway

# the other miscarriage

im outside the divine infant hospital in wakefield waiting for you oh there you are how id hover close to you & catch your eyes blinking at the cold november wind rushing at your face i would feel the fierce flares of affection & protection rise up in the ice of my veins aching to melt like lava so i could surround you with so much warmth a nuzzle of breath puffing like a cloud of steam youd know it was me long before youd understand the language of loss oh my dear twin i miss you so much already even though you arent even two days old our parents will never honor me with a name but youd feel so much love from all of us out there so many ghosts like me love all the orphans because they always end up feeling like ghosts no matter where they go so when they finally meet a real ghost like me they are rarely surprised how we are one and the same

id wonder about you every moment of my dead life like how many miles away are you now are you enjoying your time with our brothers & sisters would you have become deaf like me or would you be just hearing would you ever go swimming in the sunday lake nearby would you stop by at the pasty shop three blocks up the street from here & order your favorite pasty would you stay here after graduation or would you move away like everyone else

would mom ever tell you about me would she ever say that itd never occurred to her to name me but no i was just another miscarriage her third actually a mistake a seed shelled with abandonment no one knows why i suddenly died next to you inside the womb but if you were anything like me youd never stop pondering the shadow of me darker than midnight on north pole & the radio silence of my heartbeat emanating from the skeleton of us always dreaming the dreaming

# how to name your (dead) twin

name me
youd insist

> *i would not hug a pillow tightly to my chest aching for my missing half not an echo call from our gnarly root of veins remembering your ghost arms reaching out to embrace me way back in moms womb*

because you
didnt want

> *i would not beg for a genie over & over again to appear with a magic carpet to come take me far away from ironwood to a new family whod want to love me as i am & treat me as an equal to them even if i were deaf*

to be
left abstract

> *i would not weave through the woods across the street looking for your ghost playing hide & seek among the birches protecting me from the caveins swollen with amniotic fluid*

not a
hazy dream

> *i would not scan the lists of possible baby names because you wouldnt be just another imaginary character so how could i possibly give you a name that fits you perfectly when i dont know the life ahead of you*

nor elegy
of ache

> *i would not borrow library books featuring orphaned kids seeking a new home where a hardscrabble family would welcome them with open arms*

but alive
in flesh

*i would not leaf through my knights of the altar handbook*
*& intone the last rites of death making the sign of the cross*
*in the air over your closed eyes*

never buried
never denied

*instead on the edge of caveins where the shadow of st michaels*
*church once loomed across the water you & i would baptize*
*each other under god & be blessed forever as an ampersand*

# dream family language

if i had appreciated back then
the nuclear power of speaking up
id have told you to sit down
& let me handle this one
id tell our mom & dad i wouldnt accept their excuse
of not being able to control us kids talking all at once
id tell them that they had to set an example
too many kids hard to control dad would say
maybe but youre the father
you can stand up & tell them to shut up
& take turns & listen to each other
theyd be trained to listen to each other
a true novel skill in the hearing world
where everyone has ears but never listens
we need a new language
no more family reunions
filled with silences louder than laughter

# my other (deaf) twin

each time i visit ironwood
i pray that a rare fog will descend

seeping south from lake superior
only to evaporate into color

pulling back to reveal
the other ghost ive yet to see

who couldve played with me
up & down oak street

imprinting memories
on my fractured psyche

long enough to eradicate
the virus of loneliness

from my barren marrow
religion is no doctor

the bible is no cure
but there he is walking toward me

his face & hands would alight
crystalclear as dew clinging

to the underside of grass blades
mirroring the joy of dawn

you deaf same me hed ask in sign
of course id sign back

hed laugh yeah hearing people
full shit awful stories plenty

there under the ghost shadow of
that oak tree chopped down

years ago without warning
defacing the roths house

but now that hes found me
buildings long razed are resurrected

to show him what hed lost
from the fog clouding his life

he can see my memories rising
like phantom skyscrapers

crowding behind my back
his eyes are full of miracles

my eyes now have perfect 20 20
my glasses were never rosecolored anyway

the way he signs so clearly
i feel as if im gulping so much water

who knew family could be such a fucking desert
in the middle of wintry sundays

no one asked if i wanted a glass of clarity
i hadnt known any better with my dirty water

a little rage wouldve filtered out
its swirling obfuscation just like that

he & i may have only met but it already feels
as if centuries together will be too short

we would stand facing each other
never moving at all yet signing

laughing & telling each other the stories
we never got to tell our siblings

we are white pines taking root
our hands are full of seasons

the stories we sow
will outroot us

# fists

the boxing ring can pop up anywhere without warning

the more public the better the backyard the school the church

you two are always in training each time you discreetly observe each other
from the corners of your shared bedroom

you two never realize it but you are always coaching each other egged on
to do better than that

you two work out in the gymnasium of your family always comparing
whos more talented more beloved more rewarded

you two lace your grievances into your boxing gloves

each bloodied uppercut feels like progress

each insult feels like a jab in the guts designed to make your dreams
hemorrhage

each humiliation is a concussion fracturing the corpus callosum inside the
skull of pride

your bedroom takes on the stench of toxins releasing hurt into the air

fists clenching without the either of you saying a word is the sound of a
bell going off for another round

a look of disdain is all thats needed

## $$$$$

sure i survived but at what price
for sure it was steeper
than any down payment on any house
id have cared to own
so no home ever of my own
i was always a tenant
here were the terms of my lease with every foster family
in exchange for using their house
sitting with them at their family meals
sleeping in a room upstairs where i cant decorate
practicing fake smiles at pretend brothers
celebrating my birthdays with strangers
knowing their names but never partaking
in their own family histories
theyd just put up with me
the nasalsounding boy that i am
just be a good good boy
with those amazing hearing aids
never expect anything of anyone
in this way id learned to be afraid
of being myself with anyone
in ironwood i was awash
with nightmares of eviction
where else could i go
if my own family had made it clear
i didnt quite fit in with
the puzzle of their lives
i was a missing piece
i was too weirdly shaped
my body was too gangly worse
yet my chest started to develop swirls of fur
then my back started to grow hairy too
my exterior was starting to catch up
to the beast already growing inside
until my expensive porcelain face
fractured from the snarling
i am now a serpent tongue of hiss

# london dreaming

somewhere in the heavy
    pelt of rain & a little fog
        i crisscross portobello road
shuttling back & forth
    between stalls of bricabracs
        secondhand clothes
antique replicas
    homemade mincemeat pies
        as its cold weather
ive let my beard grow
    more salt than ginger
        to keep my face warm
i am wearing an old
    aviators jacket
        with my passport
& rfid wallet tucked
    against my breast
        a waterproof cap
pulled down to protect
    my expensive hearing aid
        a pair of thinsulate
fleece gloves
    my daypack stuffed
        with a merino wool
scarf rolled inside
    its just another day in london
        but it stops being
when i happen
    to look up & spot
        a fellow about my height
his angular face
    slightly freckled
        his lips slightly thick
his nose rather eaglelike
    his blueberry eyes
        his thinning eyebrows

his giraffe neck
 he is not beautiful
  not attractive at all
his long coat sways
 in dark herringbone
  he is wearing old sneakers
he glances at me & stops
 i glance behind me
  what could he be looking at
behind me are tourists
 with shoulder bags
  milling about
then he slows down
 walking closer
  there is something familiar
about him but what
 what my mind shouts
  my mind goes into overdrive
as he comes closer
 i slow down too
  someone stops & laughs
i dont hear the laugh
 am i seeing a ghost of myself
  the question is clear
on our faces
 how is this possible
  researchers have calculated
identical doppelgängers
 not related by blood
  are statistically almost zero
even with billions
 of people living on our planet
  soon we are standing
right in front of each other
 no mirror needed
  i dont know what to say
i am afraid he will be
 impossible to lipread
  some brits have stiff faces

would he be like that
        plus ive turned off
            my hearing aid
as is my wont when im alone
        i love earmolded silence
            so do i go ahead
& turn it back on
        but what is there to say
            hed be just another stranger
on portobello road
        we study each other
            he bursts out laughing
i glance about myself
        am i wearing something
            inappropriate or do i look
funny or weird
        do i know you i finally say
            he shakes his head no
i dont think so
        you look same as me
            yeah
you think were related like twins
        maybe
            he glances around
what year were you born
        1966 he says
            november 65 i say
i was born in america
        brighton boy here he says
            or something like that
as i havent had a chance
        to turn on my hearing aid
            so im never sure
exactly what hes said
        hasnt he noticed my nasal voice
            isnt it freaky how we
i try to finish my sentence
        but i cant
            yeah he nods

well pleasure meeting ya
    he extends his hand
        to shake mine
i will look down
    on the callouses
        coating his ice-pink hand
i will feel the cold
    in his iron poke of fingers
        even though im gloved
ill be relieved
    not twins
        at all

# holy communion

one day all of this will be found to be a preposterous dream—none of this ever happened—yet when i can see the tunnel of death awaiting to extinguish the flame of my life—i will suddenly see you—you—you will be standing on the porch peering into my living room window wondering if anyone is indeed home—youll have knocked sharply on the door demanding an answer right then & now—you will be as tall as i am—not much white hair left on your scalp just a weather-beaten harris tweed cap a hint of irish aura around you—how odd to see someone looking so much like me—how did you disappear—maybe you had been kidnapped & stolen away to live on the emerald isle running up & down the rolling hills—not many trees but what magnificent skies crisp & clear in all directions—youd have felt the pull of peat under your feet just when i pounded on the iron-dust soil in my woods across the street with my vibrations reaching your feet in a new kind of morse code yet to be invented & transcribed—youd have wondered what those sensations were for the rest of your days from boyhood on—youd have done university & become a professor all the while wondering what was missing—youd have had a wife & children—youd be a grandfather with at least six babies to dote on whenever you come down from the village—on the few times when you visited dublin or london youd spot a few deafies & stare without realizing it—for months afterward youd wonder why you had stared so—was it because they spoke in what seemed such a mysterious language—perhaps something like twinhood that mythologists & scientists have obsessed on wanting to see how the other half felt & thought as if blood itself was the magic conduit—telepathy is the nectar of those aching to worship their missing halves—yes your grandchildren would carry on your last name but something would have long felt missing from your marrow—something like a hole in the ground not yours not mine but something else—no name no thesaurus to triangulate its boundaries—not the dampness in the air—maybe a sheaf of doctored paperwork would come tumbling out of a box long overlooked in the attic—you would see the stark facts that your adoptive parents have never shared your original name your place of birth—youd suddenly feel aflame with purpose perhaps flying to america a country you found strange always on each trip youd taken to attend an academic conference or two—suddenly the hole in the ground would have a shape—a name—werent you always what you were told you were—but now theres a strange last name—luczak—how do you pronounce that—edward john luczak—your father—lorraine eleanor luczak—your mother—youd show up at the courthouse in bessemer michigan—youd overhear the court clerks startlement looks like you werent the only one born that day—what youd gasp what—looks like you got yourself a twin brother oh wow lookit that oh shit i cant tell you his name for legal reasons—youd stand with your knees ready to buckle—how was this possible—youd eventually learn that our parents have died a long time ago—youd never know the struggles ive had with our mother how she

ONCE UPON A TWIN

didnt want me to be deaf or gay how she didnt want me to sign or talk about men—no more special rights she said im tired of special groups expecting special rights—she never saw my point how she had already more rights than i—only that i wanted only the same rights as she—youd seek out your longlost siblings—would they believe you—would they welcome you as one of their own just like how my sister marys best friend laurie was—shes been accepted like a sister to all of us though not of blood & yet i am not accepted in spite of my blood—would they flock like bees around a pot of honey the newness of you as family in their midst all the while ignoring my existence—would you understand how orphaned ive been all my life—would you want them as much as i dont want them—would you see clearly how theyre not my family—or maybe youd seek me out instead wondering about your missing half—youd download one book after another exploring the phenomena of missing twins—how they somehow intuit each other without quite knowing about their lost half a continent away—then youd remember those odd sensations in your feet—youd stamp your feet on the ground hoping to signal a message back to me in my woods—but ill be on my deathbed already for isnt that how life works—you have to wait until the very end before the story of your life makes any big picture sense—id be looking up from my living room startled to see a ghost of myself—has mr death arrived—no id think im not ready—ive got so much more to do im not done yet—there are still untold stories left in my blood—i can see ghosts flickering in the far fields of my peripheral vision but im not ready to turn my head to look squarely at them—to do so is to die—no

no no—whos that man peering into my living room window—youd look

strangely like me but you wouldnt dress like me—what the hell do you

want—wracked with pain in my hips id groan push myself up on a gnarly

oak cane hobble across the well-worn woolen rug & open the door just to

make sure you were for real—you wouldnt disappear—you wouldnt say a

word—id be speechless too—i wouldnt know who you were but i wouldnt

need your name to know the most important fact of my life long shielded

by our parents—we once belonged to each other—we held each other for

nine months—the veins of our hearts once braided inside the womb of

our church where we worshiped—we had breathed in each others scent—

without saying another word wed fall into an embrace—no matter how

old weve become no matter how different our bodies have become since we

last held each other our bodies would lock perfectly key in hole—wed hold

each other & sob—wed blather nonsense—doesnt matter what we were

saying—what would matter was that we were hearing each others voice for

the first time—wed stop & wipe our snot off our sleeves—id invite you

right into my house—youd sit opposite me—the sun behind you would

turn you into a silhouette—youd be impossible to lipread but id still

hear just enough to know not your exact words but the meaning of your

words—how could anyone keep us apart—we are twins—we are bloody

twins youd keep saying like a mantra—how could our bloody parents do

this to us—wed speculate maybe they couldnt afford you—maybe you were sold for money—youd walk over to my sofa & hold my hand—wed look at each other & just laugh—youd keep saying were fucking bloody twins—id suddenly weep—my town my church my house—my pearl onion my lima bean my petite pea—my diamond my pebble my atom—in the womb of my death i long to find you waiting for me with your needle ready to sew both helixes of our dna back together—no more fucking stories except the one about us finally coming home to each other

houghton
(1974–1976)

## todd w carlborn

he said hed wait for me
when i came back from
my oneonone catechism class
with a beadyeyed nun
with a turkey wattle neck
at st ignatius loyola school
on the other side of the canal
it was for only one hour
but i came back on the van
there he was waiting on the playground
we were in third grade
seeing him smiling
i didnt know that there were many kinds of love
i didnt know that i could be
allowed to feel love
so many people had manipulated me
into doing so many unwanted things
maybe because i wore hearing aids
& had to do speech therapy
but he never demanded anything
he stood there smiling & waiting
on some winter nights i thought of him
when i peered out from my window
overlooking the valley
with the portage lift bridge on my left
& michigan tech on my far right
& mont ripley ski hill straight ahead
at night the skiers wore headlights
to weave blurs of light down the slope
his backyard was near the foot of the ski hill
i never saw his house itself
i knew it was somewhere on royce road
because id looked up his address
in the phone book at the house
where i was staying
in houghton during the week
but which house i never knew

i imagined his house to be a sad brown affair
its black shingles with asphalt siding hung in rows
its nails slowly rusting underneath
its black tar hiding the darkness of men & women
divorce happened in that house
he was the first person i knew who had divorced parents
he never went into details
just fighting all the time he said
just like how i never told him
about that one friday night
when i came home to ironwood from houghton
i found dad all blustered up & so angry
that he pulled out a long white rubbery tube
already flayed
he had to whup someones ass
i was too scared to watch
i heard someone yelp
we were all silenced
i never learned the details
of what happened earlier in the week
while i was gone
i turned silent all weekend
my father became a ghost with sad sad sad eyes
i dont recall him asking for forgiveness
a cloud of fear hung invisibly
my eight brothers & sisters eventually started
laughing & carrying on
as if nothing happened
but i never forgot the whip
its splayed ends tucked between
the two stacks of newspapers
atop the refrigerator
i never asked todd why his parents fought
that never mattered to me
he was simply a boy who stood waiting for me
unlike my siblings who nodded hi
whenever i came home for the weekend
after five days away in houghton
he made me feel worth waiting for

ONCE UPON A TWIN

# charles e klingbeil

even back in third grade
chuck was taller & bigger
than anyone in our class

i was becoming more & more
mainstreamed in my hearing class
i was to sit in the front row

& lipread ms rhodehaven
todd probably sat near me
we had our art classes

in the basement of ryan school
it wasnt designed to be a classroom
probably a former storage room

it had a quadrant of four tables
chuck & his buddies took one table
todd & i with a few others took another

during a lull when the teacher had to step
out for a minute chuck nudged his friends
he made a dirty face at me

i didnt say anything it was the first time
a hearing classmate had made fun of me
todd suddenly said something

id never seen him so angry
i was afraid to ask what hed just said
chuck & his buddies just cracked up

the coals of fury in todds eyes
never cooled
even when the teacher returned

*

returning to houghton as a sophomore
i unexpectedly recognized chuck
in the hallway between classes

impossibly taller & bigger
with broad shoulders
id never seen a boy my age

strut or bulk up that big
my ironwood catholic high school
didnt have a football team

chuck was my first boyman
not a boy not a teenager
not yet a man but an aura

of what he would become
he didnt seem to recognize me
he was apparently big on football

in our classroom he never registered
on my radar i wasnt afraid of him at all
these jocks were never my friends

*

the rules of football have always been
beyond my comprehension
so on a big green field of white stripes

a whistle startles & then
a football is tossed some yards
then bam a mass of arms legs & helmets

& all for what more brain concussions
now that chuck has died suddenly
a heart attack at ohare airport

i google for images of him my jaw drops
he was a nfl player really wow
he had played for the miami dolphins

anyway he had a knee injury or something
got addicted to heavy painkillers
had been using anabolic steroids too

ended up coaching at michigan tech
made a few drugaddled miscalculations
stood up & responded to the judge

well my thinking got me here
hey chuck i forgive you
too late to say that now but yeah

# my first phone call

when i lived on east houghton avenue
thc house was usually empty after school
ace had died the summer before
the ghost of him still trailed after me
but i would be a strong boy
i would not be a crybaby

the chambers lived in that house
big & brown & three stories high
plus a basement that always felt chilly
larry & marge had a small bedroom
with their own bathroom
i was given their daughters bedroom
she was away at college in north dakota
tim lived in the room next door to me
marc lived up in the attic
a college student rented the other attic room
whom i rarely saw
the kitchen was small
the dining room was three times as big
with a view of mont ripley right across the canal

anyway todds last name was in the phone book
it was the first number i ever memorized
the chambers had a phone on the second floor
centrally located between the bathroom
larry & marges master bedroom
tims room
then my room that was really debbies room
whenever the phone rang
you never knew who was going to pop
out of the rooms on that floor
i always kept an eye out whenever
that sound echoed in my ears

one day after school
i had my usual grape jelly on crackers

i had no dog to pet & chase
when anyone was home
they didnt talk much to me
they were too busy during the day
larry was michigan techs vice president
marge was studying to become a realtor
marc was a college student at michigan tech
tim was a high school student
i was in fourth grade

id never made a phone call before
i didnt warn todd i was gonna call
i simply wanted to know what it felt like
to hook my finger into the circle plate of holes
& push down those numbers
4 . . . 8 . . . 2 . . .
the phone was avocado green
never saw a phone in that color before

i held the receiver to my ear
it never occurred to me
to swing it down to my chest
where my hearing aids were
i thought i heard a ringing
wait was that a click
frightened i hung up

i thought the police would come swarming
their bright red lights cutting through the heavy snowfall
their dark uniforms clambering down the long sidewalk
to the front door pounding for entry
they would pinpoint me trying not to cry
even if id squirreled away way up in the attic
in the tiny storage cubbyhole
but i didnt move
i stayed where i was on that chair
looking through the front window
watching the whiteness of snow
turn into a monochrome gray
as the night held its breath

waiting for the phone to ring back
with him not saying anything
because he knew how
i didnt need to hear his voice
to know he was my best friend

## that 1 jet hockey game

todd you unexpectedly reappeared
at my house in ironwood
one december evening
a year after i was transferred back home
to ironwood catholic grade school
two hours drive away from you
teachers & parents had felt
i would be a real mainstreamed success
& closer to my family too
no one seemed to care
how much work it took me
to lipread even with my hearing aids

                    but anyway there you stood
                       you were a bit taller
                    so was i but in those days
              nobody was sending off warning bells
                    about the onset of puberty
                      you wore a button shirt
                   you met some of my siblings
                     who were watching tv
                        & my mom too
                    maybe you met my dad too
               your divorced dad had relocated
            back to ironwood so you were visiting him
               he didnt live too far from my house
                     just over the hill actually
                 though i didnt know it at the time

so there you were with your impish smile
when we went downstairs to play jet hockey
i wanted to tell you about them boys
at my new school who had figured out
ways to make me cry so they could laugh
at my nasal voice missing consonants
& my earmolds standing out like buttons
waiting to be pressed only in my nightmares

i wanted to tell you how badly i missed you
each time i stood by the brick wall
watching them boys play nerf football
i wanted to tell you how much
i wanted to run away from home
& hide in your bedroom off royce road
so nobody but you would find me
i would be your ghost friend
alive but never dead
always looking out for you


                                        instead we stood facing each other
on either side of the big jet hockey console

                                        its blue & red markings printed
on the formica ice of a hockey rink
                        punctured with holes to let air rise

allowing the flapjack puck
                                        to float across the sheen surface

                        as if an ufo zigzagging

                                                we played the game so hard
with our round handsticks

                        the puck sometimes flew straight up
& slapped the low ceiling above us

                                        we laughed so hard it was as if
                nothing between us had changed

                                        & yet everything had

oh todd i lied about everything
                        cause i didnt want you to worry

# raymond a krumm

at ryan school todd & i had desks
next to each other as we watched mr krumm

our fourthgrade teacher stand tall
with wispy dark hair & a mustache

he wore dark ties pale shirts & cardigans
we didnt know hed only begun teaching

if hed felt any hesitation in dealing
with a large classroom full of kids

he never showed it he smiled & carried on
with whatever he had to teach us

but someone sitting in the back
threw a crack about todd

i didnt know what hed said
just a crackle of laughter from behind

i thought for a moment hed said
something mean about me

i turned to todd he looked ready to cry
then i realized it wasnt about me

mr krumm said something sharp
the kids in the back quieted down

then it was recess time he looked at todd
when the classroom emptied out

it was just him todd & me
mr krumm spoke quietly & slowly

he explained that at one time
he was a fat boy too

but when he got older he lost his fat
he didnt have to wear husky pants anymore

he looked at todd so one day
itll happen to you too just wait

i turned to todd & felt incredulous
i never thought of him as fat or chubby

i spotted a new look on todds face
i didnt understand what it meant

years later when todd & i met again
he had spent some years in the navy

so he ran his own home improvement
business in virginia beach

he came out as bisexual &
moved in with a blond hairdresser

i couldnt believe how handsome
todd looked with his mustache

it was then mr krumm flashed in my mind
i asked todd if he remembered our teacher

he nodded with a laugh oh god
i used to have a big crush on him

i said you look a lot like him now
he said really then im happy

## mere boys

one cold october afternoon
by the swing set
i showed todd
a small drawing
only two by three inches
id made with a pen
of a penis & testicles
its shriveled texture
hanging like fruits
covered with spiky hairs
i no longer remember why
i drew the image
i also no longer remember why
i decided to show him
the drawing
right there in the yard
while other kids
ran past us
he burst out
laughing
he couldnt believe
my audacity
in drawing
something like that
were we already aware
by fourth grade
that faggotry wasnt cool
either way he didnt
change at all
never shied away
never talked me down
never strayed away
we were still boys
hes dead now
how i long to ask him
if he remembers
that drawing

hey todd come unto me i pray
tell me what you remember
repeat if you must
so i never have
to doubt myself again

kyrie

# double helix kyrie
*in english and asl gloss*

| | |
|---|---|
| its still hard to enunciate | *explain difficult-difficult whew* |
| *ghosts talk how-how* | the language of ghosts |
| not easy to master | *learn fingersnaps can't* |
| *context none* | subtexts with no context |
| its glossary is impossible | *g-l-o-s-s-a-r-y impossible* |
| *me life complain-complain list* | im a catalog of grievances |
| but i want forgiveness | *but me want forgive-forgive still* |
| *mistake-mistake long-ago* | in my concordances |
| im a jumble | *my try speak-speak* |
| *find mouth gibberish-gibberish* | of nonsensical idioms |
| even vowels have | *v-o-w-e-l-s speak-speak* |
| *can't impossible* | vanished from my tongue |
| whats left are my hands | *left what hands-these* |
| *grab s-h-a-d-o-w experience* | having captured shadow itself |
| & breaking free in the sun | *stand wide-open sun fall-on-face* |

*one day world over o-r-p-h-a-n-s* one day all orphans of the world

will gather not in rage & sorrow *gather together will angry sad not*

*but all-us together warm out* but in that hazy aura

of loneliness standing *stand lonely where*

*b-r-i-c-k wall west a-r-c-h street* by the brick wall on west arch street

where i once stood & *me long-ago stand alone*

*envision revenge* daydreamed revenge

my wings of sin are heavy *my wings heavy why me sin finish*

*rage constant-constant enough not* rage alone isn't enough fuel

to enable me to fly *wings-fly can't*

*still all-us o-r-p-h-a-n-s* together these orphans & i

will nod slowly to each other *nod-nod-nod-each-other*

*stand-in-rows-move-together* together we will walk as one

through each city in the world *each city world touch-touch-touch*

*people out-there recognize will* people shall hear our massive silence

the most powerful sound *silence power strong*

*loud noise not-matter* no matter how anyone tries

| | |
|---|---|
| grief is untranslatable | *grief translate-translate impossible* |
| *grief force-us ready not* | we learn it when we dont want to |
| moving as one | *stand-in-rows-move-together* |
| *shout-shout for-for* | we dont have to shout epithets |
| our stories will carry in the air | *individual story-story float-swirl-up* |
| *same-same wind-wind north* | just like the north winds |
| gusting about | *gust-gust* |
| *wind-wind enter-our-mouths* | they only have to breathe us in |
| for that kick of memory | *us-awaken remember wow* |
| *me ghost happen body have finish* | im just a ghost made of flesh |
| who shouldve belonged | *hearing family fit-right-in should* |
| *but my story unique not* | but you know what happened |
| i got stuck in the mucky rut | *me stuck same-old-same-old* |
| *between life death choose which* | between alive & dead |
| lies & more lies | *hearing family lie-lie build-build-up* |
| *you twin mine dark bright* | my dear half my shadow my light |
| youre not a ghost youre alive | *you ghost not you body have* |

*suffer-suffer yours mine same*    your osmium past is mine

let me absolve you of its weight    *come-here me-take burden-off*

*cry-cry here-shoulder go-ahead*    please cry onto my shoulder

you can cry all you want    *fine cry-cry fine okay*

*you twin mine cherish-deep*    oh damn my dear twin

why did you have to miscarry    *accident-birth happen why?*

*you stand-stand eyes-transfixed*    i still see you standing before me

i would never let you go    *connect-together let-go never*

*if happen me die*    until the very end of my days

when the heavens crack    *heavens ceiling crack-open*

*sun ray-falling-down*    open with a beam of light

floodlighting your face    *your face bright*

*you age never*    forever ageless

our feet already on that ladder    *double-helix ready climb*

*memory telepathy*    signaling memory to come

we would climb rising together    *us-two stand-rise-together*

*arms-around-each-other*    as one in fetal embrace

our petal cells dividing   *f-e-t-u-s open-up-flower*

*c-e-l-l-s divide-divide-up-around*   a trillion times over

until we are whole again   *become one-one meet-become one*

*birth again*   newly born

signing & singing   *us-two sign-sing-sign-sing*

*us-two language one finish*   in a language only our own

## the conflation of memory: an afterword

A memory can feel so sharply rendered that it must be concrete, real; close enough to be considered factual, indisputable.

Yet, as you may recall from this book's first poem "9 months," my mother kept changing details about the third miscarriage she'd undergone in the spring of 1965. For a long time I felt perplexed over which version of the story to believe as authoritative.

But I was never confused about my longing for a comrade who would've made my childhood in Ironwood less hellish. The ache to feel loved and accepted as part of my hearing family inspired this book. Its language is deliberately incomplete because I have always felt incomplete in their midst. I am a nonperson who gets a little conversation from my siblings (with one exception), and that's it. Regardless of what they may say with words, their actions have spoken much louder. I do not really matter at all.

*

The poems in this book do not mention a key reason why I'd felt sure in my bones that I *had* to be a twin: I had an aunt and uncle who were twins. Uncle Bernard died a prisoner of war in World War II; he was only 23 years old. Aunt Bernice went on to marry the man who would become my godfather. I have never heard her talk about her lost twin. Not once. They were apparently very close.

But I didn't learn anything more about Uncle Bernard. He was one of the many sepia-toned faces that glittered among a sea of photographs propped up in the dining room at my grandmother's house.

You see, in a large hearing family like mine, no one sits down to explain family stories directly to you, because they are often shared spontaneously around the kitchen table, which I of course couldn't always follow. I don't have that scrapbook of family legends to bind me to them; all I have left are fragments that do not always connect.

*

For years I'd always thought my maternal grandmother had died of a stroke on a Tuesday: October 22, 1977. The poem "gods copper" tells the story of how I became a writer but with a key omission. Mrs. Fraites, a speech therapist (and, ironically enough, my best friend at Ironwood Catholic Grade School), had assigned me a new kind of homework the day before my grandmother's stroke: Mrs. Fraites thought I should try writing a few limericks. They were due on the following Monday.

I remember going to my grandmother's burial and going to class not long after since the Ironwood Catholic Grade School was only two blocks away from the cemetery. This happened on a Friday. (My mother said that my memory of going to school right after burial couldn't be accurate because everyone would've been expected to go back to church right after the burial for the funeral reception.)

Then on the Sunday after, I suddenly remembered my speech homework due the next day. I sat down and tried to write a limerick about a witch in a ditch. Something inside me clicked. I've never stopped writing since.

Some months ago I asked my mother if she happened to have a copy of my grandmother's obituary. It was then we made a startling discovery. She did die on October 22, but it happened on a Saturday! My mother then remembered how my grandmother had hoped to be buried on a good-weather day so everyone from out of town could come to her funeral.

My mother had also thought she'd died on a Tuesday, so she went to the county courthouse for a look at her death certificate. Yes, she did pass away on a Saturday, not Tuesday. The funeral couldn't possibly have happened on a Friday!

That my mind was blown is an understatement. How could we have so misremembered all those years? Why did both our memories conflate two different events—the stroke and death—as if they'd happened on the same day? And why did I ever think that I went to class after the burial?

Most puzzling, indeed!

*

The day when I got the contract for the publication of this book was also the day that I got a most unexpected note from my mother via snail mail.

The small envelope contained a note she'd written to herself back in 1965. She has always kept meticulous notes about doctor appointments and the like in her impeccable handwriting on pieces of scrap paper. As a child of the Great Depression, she knew how to be thrifty. She never threw out scrap paper while we kids were growing up. If we wanted to draw or make paper hats, she always pointed to the upper drawer of a small white cabinet sandwiched between the refrigerator and stove where a huge pile of paper awaited us.

Her note showed information I hadn't known before: when I was born, I weighed six pounds, six ounces. Six weeks later I weighed nine pounds, twelve ounces. But right above that information was a startling inscription: "MISCARRIAGE 1-15-65." (I was born in November 1965.)

Did this mean that I had never been a twin at all? If that was the case, how could my mother have been *so* confused over the timing of her miscarriage?

Memory can be such a wily trickster.

*

I've always thought myself as a poet–photographer. I treat each poetry collection as a series of snapshots delineating how I'd thought and felt about a given topic at a certain time. *once upon a twin* is no different in this regard; I had truly believed for the longest time that I was a twin.

I pray that long after I'm gone, my work as a whole will be seen as a long-running scrapbook of my life, and that others who aren't accepted by their own biological families will find in me a kindred sibling.

# acknowledgments

The author wishes to thank the following people who've enabled (or inspired) this book to happen in one way or another, both seemingly trivial and large: Sibel Cedetas, John Lee Clark, David Cummer, Arthur Durkee, Scott Holl, Raymond Krumm, Stephen Kuusisto, Katie Lee, Angela Leppig, Lorraine Luczak, Vivien Arielle Luczak, Eric Thomas Norris, Mary Ruefle, Ellen McGrath Smith, Tom Steele, Connie Voisine, and all the editors who've chosen his odd poems for inclusion in their journals.

The following poems, a few of which have been revised since, appeared in these publications:

*ArLiJo*: "my corpse self."
*Brain Mill Press* (Editors' Pick for BMP Poetry Month): "9 months."
*The Chaffin Journal*: "charles e klingbeil."
*Into the Void*: "the other night when i died."
*Inverted Syntax*: "gods copper" (nominated for a Best of the Net award).
*Killjoy Magazine*: "atonement."
*Lunch Ticket*: "deaf rich boy 79."
*Nine Mile*: "my first phone call."
*OutWrite Festival Journal 2019*: "if my twin were a she."
*Poetry*: "double helix kyrie."
*Rogue Agent*: "fraternal identical."
*SOFTBLOW*: "$$$$$."
*Strukturriss*: "my other (deaf) twin."
*The Thing Itself*: "dream family language."
*Total Eclipse*: "first prayer."
*Verity La*: "braided veins."
*We Are Not Your Metaphor: A Disability Poetry Anthology* (Zoeglossia Fellows, ed.; Squares & Rebels): "todd w carlborn."
*Wordgathering*: "battle preparations," "heretics" (originally titled "mortal sin"), and "that 1 jet hockey game."

# about the author

Raymond Luczak lost most of his hearing at the age of eight months due to double pneumonia and a high fever, but this was not detected until he was two-and-a-half years old. After all, he was just number seven in a hearing family of nine children growing up in Ironwood, a small mining town in Michigan's Upper Peninsula. Forbidden to sign, he was outfitted with a rechargeable hearing aid and started on speech therapy immediately. Because there were no programs for deaf children in Ironwood, he was brought two hours away to a speech therapy program in Houghton where he would live with three foster families for a total of nine years.

Luczak is the author and editor of more than twenty books, including *Flannelwood: A Novel*, *QDA: A Queer Disability Anthology*, and *Compassion, Michigan: The Ironwood Stories*. His other titles include *From Heart into Art: Interviews with Deaf and Hard of Hearing Artists and Their Allies* and the award-winning Deaf gay novel *Men with Their Hands*. He currently edits the literary journal *Mollyhouse*. An inaugural Zoeglossia Fellow and a eleven-time Pushcart Prize nominee, he lives in Minneapolis, Minnesota.